TAKE A
MOMENT

TAKE A MOMENT

Activities to Refocus, Recentre and Relax Wherever You Are

Illustrated by Sophie Richardson

In aid of

All royalties from the sale of this book (a minimum of £10,000) will be donated to Mind, a registered charity in England and Wales (charity number 219830)

Michael O'Mara Books Limited

First published in Great Britain in 2019
by Michael O'Mara Books Limited
9 Lion Yard, Tremadoc Road
London SW4 7NQ

A CIP catalogue record for this book is available from the British Library.

Papers used by Michael O'Mara Books Limited are natural, recyclable products made from wood grown in sustainable forests. The manufacturing processes conform to the environmental regulations of the country of origin.

ISBN: 978-1-78929-038-7 in paperback print format

1 2 3 4 5 6 7 8 9 10

www.mombooks.com

Illustrated by Sophie Richardson www.studiosophie.co.uk
Cover design by Claire Cater
Typeset by Barbara Ward

Printed and bound in China

This book belongs to:

_____

_____

Introduction

You matter. Your wellbeing matters. But when life's busy (and even when it's not), we could all do with a bit of help prioritizing ourselves as we go about our day. Developed in partnership with Mind, the mental health charity, *Take a Moment* is here to do just that. It's here for when you need a break – whenever, wherever – just five minutes to yourself, for yourself. Whether you need to decompress, refocus or just relax, there is a variety of techniques and exercises in this book that will provide you with instant expert support and inspiration on the go.

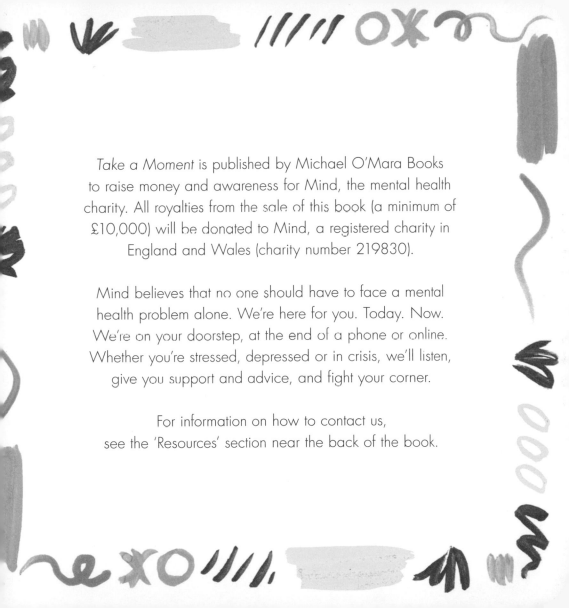

Turn Down the Noise

Our world can be full of 'noise', whether it's text messages buzzing, washing machines beeping, social media feeds lighting up our screens, or even just the hubbub of a busy home or office. All of them clamour for our attention, many insisting that we immediately get on with the next 'must-do' in our day. Being surrounded by such distractions and interruptions can make it hard to focus, make decisions or even just fully relax. Simply removing yourself from this noise, even if it's just for five or ten minutes, can help.

Find a quiet (it doesn't need to be silent),
safe space where you aren't likely to be disturbed,
and for five minutes (or longer, if you can) turn off your
phone. Not just on silent or flight mode, but *off* off.
If possible, leave your phone in a different room.

Being in a quiet space without distractions may
feel strange or uncomfortable at first, in which case
you could use this time to try one of the relaxation
techniques in this book (such as the breathing exercise
on the following page). And if you can't be in a quiet
place straight away, think of a space that could
work and then plan for when you can be there.

Focus on Breathing

When we feel overwhelmed, it's often not just our mind but our body, too, that gets in on the act. This breathing exercise can be a great first step to refocusing your mind and calming your body at the same time.

1. Find a quiet, safe space where you can sit, stand or lie comfortably.

2. If you're lying down, position your arms so that they aren't touching your sides, to give your chest room to expand.

3. If you're sitting or standing, place both feet flat on the floor, roughly hip-width apart.

4. As you breathe in, allow the air to flow deep inside you, but don't force it. It should feel comfortable.

5. While breathing in, it can be helpful to count steadily from one to five. Don't worry if at first you can't reach five, it should get a bit easier as you keep going.

6. Without pausing or holding your breath, breathe out. Again, this can be done to the count of five.

7. Keep doing this for five minutes.

Leave Your Thoughts
on the Page

If, when trying to relax, you find that your mind keeps whirring with everyday thoughts or worries, doing this exercise first may be helpful.

1. Sit quietly for a minute and just notice the thoughts that are going through your mind.

2. Can you separate out the different thoughts?

3. As you notice each one, write them down on the following pages – or you could draw them, if you prefer. Don't hurry.

4. When you feel that you have pinpointed as many as you can and put them down on paper, you might choose to read them back to yourself or you may decide just to leave them where they are. Alternatively, instead of writing them here, you could write them down on strips of paper and then rip them up.

5. Whatever you choose to do, the next step is to decide consciously that, just for a little while, you will leave these thoughts here. Now pick one of the relaxation exercises in this book to do for the next five or ten minutes (or longer, if you want).

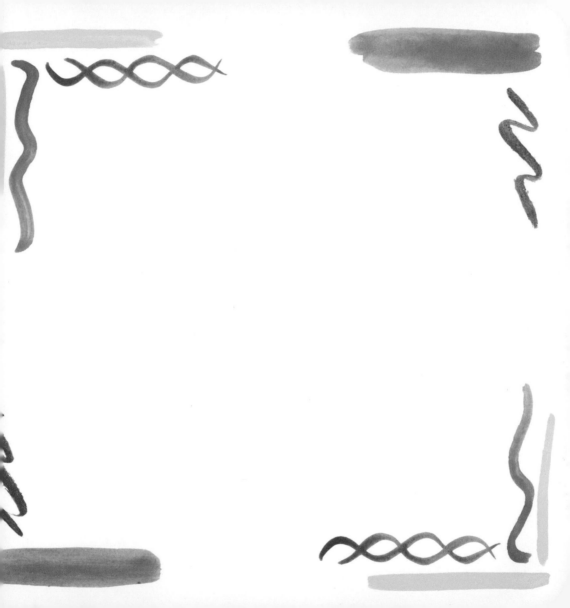

'The greatest weapon against stress is our ability to choose one thought over another.'

William James

Daily Self-Care

Think now about what simple, everyday things you
could do to care for yourself. These aren't necessarily
just things that you enjoy doing (although they should
certainly be that too), but rather things that nourish you and
actively prioritize you and your needs. It might be taking
a bath, going for a walk around the local park, making
yourself a nutritious meal or snack, meditating or listening
to an audio book or podcast.

Is there something that you could do right now
to prioritize yourself and your wellbeing?
If you need inspiration, there are lots of ideas
in this book to start you off.

Helping Others

Once we've had practice at caring for ourselves,
we're often in a better position to help and support
others. Research has also shown that committing
regular acts of kindness is associated with an increase
in wellbeing, meaning everyone benefits.

Is there something you could do right now to show
support to someone in your life? It might be as simple
as texting a friend or family member to tell them
that you're thinking of them, or making
a cup of coffee for a colleague.

Stretch to Destress #1

When we feel stressed, we often hold tension in our body. Releasing that tension by stretching can be a simple way to help us feel calmer and more relaxed. These stretches can all be done while you're sitting down, so you can easily fit them into your day, and each one focuses on a different part of the body – this one helps to stretch out the back of your arms. If you'd like to try others, flip forward in the book.

1. Sit or stand with your back straight and plant both feet flat on the floor, roughly hip-width apart.

2. Raise both arms above your head.

3. Bend your left arm and allow your hand to reach across to your right arm and drop down, so that the elbow is bent and loose.

4.   Now with your right hand, grasp your left elbow and gently pull it towards your head.

5.   Hold the position for ten to thirty seconds, or for however long is comfortable.

6.   Let go of your elbow, allowing both arms to come down and slowly return to your sides.

7.   Now repeat for the other side.

Remember to breathe normally while you stretch and don't go further than is comfortable for you. If you find this stretch too difficult, there are others in the book you could try.

'The gift is to the giver, and comes back most to him – it cannot fail.'

Walt Whitman

Take Note of Your Feelings

Our feelings determine so much about how we experience our day-to-day lives. Yet many of us don't actively pay attention to them.

Spend five minutes now checking in with how you are feeling. As you go, try not to judge your feelings, but rather approach them with a sense of curiosity and compassion.

What words best describe how you are feeling right now? For example, are you calm, frustrated, angry, tense, sad, bored, content?

How intense are each of these feelings?

Are they loud or more like background noise?

What sensations are you experiencing in your body?

Are there any other feelings that you weren't
initially aware of?

Once you are aware of how you are feeling,
remind yourself again to approach your feelings with
compassion. Depending on what this experience was like
for you, you may want to follow it with another exercise,
such as 'What Do I Need Right Now?' or 'Barefoot'.

Express It Without Words

Words are not the only way to express how we feel.
And sometimes it can help to try another method.

Use the page opposite to express how you are feeling
right now. It can be with shapes, colours, pictures,
whatever. As you think about each feeling and what
it might look like, try to observe and accept it with
friendly curiosity and without judgement.

What Do I Need Right Now?

Sometimes, when we feel stressed or under pressure (and even when we don't), it can be hard to make decisions. You may feel that there are hundreds of things that need doing or that what lies ahead of you is too big to scale. The point of this exercise is to focus on your needs in this moment, right now.

Wherever you are, stop and think about: 'What one thing would support my wellbeing *right now*?' It might be finishing an email you're in the middle of, having lunch, putting the recycling out, getting home safely. It might be that what *you need* is to take a break for five minutes. Or it might be smaller than that. Perhaps it's getting up to put the kettle on. Once you have that one thing clear in your mind, go and do it.

If you find it hard to focus on what your needs are in this moment, perhaps try the simple breathing exercise, 'Focus on Breathing', near the beginning of this book first.

'Knowing yourself
is the beginning
of all wisdom.'

Aristotle

Plan Your Next Break

You may not be able to take a break whenever you need one, but it's important to have some time that's yours. If you don't have the space right now, make a plan for when you will. Give yourself enough time to really benefit from the rest. If you can, aim for half an hour to an hour. To help make the most of the break, plan to do something relaxing, such as taking a bath, sitting down with a cup of tea, or reading a book or magazine.

Perhaps consider making this a regular break every day or every other day. If you keep a diary or planner, schedule it in with a note to remind yourself.

Shrug It Off

If you find yourself in a situation where you can't easily take a break, you can use this very simple and short stretching exercise not only to relieve tension from your shoulders and neck, but also as an opportunity to prioritize your wellbeing. It can be done anytime, anywhere, seated or standing.

1. Gently lift your shoulders up towards your ears.

2. Hold them up for two seconds.

3. Let them fall slowly, gently rolling them back or forward as you relax down.

4. You should feel tension being released as your shoulders drop.

Repeat eight to ten times (or however many times you want), alternating rolling your shoulders back and forward on the way down.

Support Plan

There are times in life when we all need help, when our own
internal resources feel depleted and life becomes a struggle.
If you can see that there is a stressful or difficult period
ahead, it can help to prepare for it so that you can have
a plan to turn to when you need it.

Think about what regular commitments you could reduce,
for example social activities or workload.

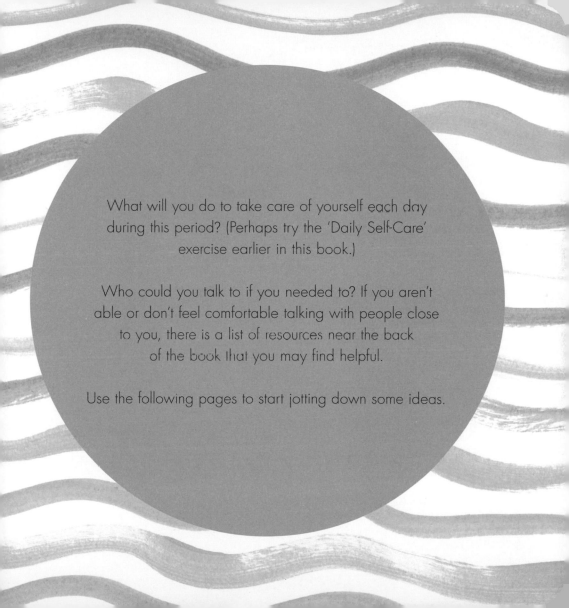

What will you do to take care of yourself each day during this period? (Perhaps try the 'Daily Self-Care' exercise earlier in this book.)

Who could you talk to if you needed to? If you aren't able or don't feel comfortable talking with people close to you, there is a list of resources near the back of the book that you may find helpful.

Use the following pages to start jotting down some ideas.

'Take rest;
a field that has rested
gives a bountiful crop.'

Ovid

Happiness Box

Create a happiness box. And we don't just mean an imaginary one. When our mood drops, it can take our energy, motivation and creativity with it. Having something real and solid that you can turn to when you're feeling too low to come up with ideas can make a real difference.

Find a box and fill it with things that cheer you up. You could include your favourite book or film, a notebook and pen to write down your thoughts or words of encouragement to yourself (see the following exercise 'Dear Future Me'). You could even keep this book in there.

Dear Future Me

Take this opportunity to write a note to your future self.
Think about what you'd like Future You to know.
How might you reassure or encourage them?

Think about different scenarios when some words of
comfort might be of help. For instance, you could write
a note to include in your 'Happiness Box' (see the
previous page). Or perhaps you're heading for a stressful
event where you might feel in need of some support.

If you've got a bit more time, you could try writing
yourself a longer letter on the following pages.

'Things which matter the most must never be at the mercy of things which matter least.'

Johann Wolfgang von Goethe

Mindful Hydration

This is a really simple exercise, involving nothing more than a glass of water. It's best done when you have a few minutes to yourself and also when you are not feeling really thirsty. Take each step very slowly, allowing your mind to be absorbed by your different senses.

1. Pour yourself a glass of water.

2. Before you take a sip, let your attention rest on the glass.

3. Look at how the water sits in the glass, how the light reflects upon the different surfaces.

4. Feel the glass's smoothness and shape. Notice its temperature.

5. When you bring the glass to your mouth, notice how it feels against your lips.

6. Slowly take a sip of water and hold it in your mouth.

7. Notice any subtle flavours or sensations on your tongue.

8. Notice how the water changes temperature in your mouth.

9. When you swallow the water, think about how the water is flowing through your body, hydrating and replenishing it.

10. Once you have swallowed the water, take a slow, deep breath and start again.

11. Try doing this exercise for five or ten minutes, and then finish any remaining water.

If you find your attention wandering, just notice where it has gone before gently bringing it back to the glass of water.

You can do this exercise with other drinks if you prefer; it can be helpful to vary the experience with different colours and flavours.

Stretch to Destress #2

This exercise helps stretch out the muscles in your back, sides and arms, gently releasing any tension that may have built up there.

1. Sit or stand with your back straight and plant both feet flat on the floor, roughly hip-width apart.

2. Raise both arms above your head and interlock your fingers, with the palms facing out.

3. Push your arms towards the ceiling, stretching upwards and allowing your shoulders to rise with them.

4. Hold the position for ten to thirty seconds, or for however long is comfortable.

5. Unlock your fingers, slowly sweep your arms back down and return them to your sides.

6. If you can, do this stretch a couple more times.

Remember to breathe normally while you stretch and don't go further than is comfortable for you. If you find this stretch too difficult, there are others in the book you could try.

Break It Down

Whether it's cleaning out the loft, getting a new job or just leaving the house, some things can feel overwhelming. Many of us have heard of the advice to break down difficult projects into more manageable chunks, but even knowing where to start can be hard. This exercise will help you make a plan when you don't know how or where to begin.

1. Get a pad of sticky notes (or you could rip up a piece of paper into small bits) and a pen.

2. Think about the project ahead and quickly write on a sticky note just one step that needs to be completed in order to accomplish the project.

3. If when you write it down that step still feels daunting, break it down even further into two or more further steps and write these down instead.

4. Now think of another step that needs to get done and write that down on another sticky note. Don't worry about the order at this point. Keep going until you've run out of ideas.

5. Select two of the sticky notes and look at the steps that you've written down. Place them both on the table or floor in front of you. Which one needs to happen first? Put that one above the other.

6. Pick up another sticky note. Compare it to the two you've already placed in front of you. Does it need to happen before, after or in between these steps? Place the note in its position.

7. Continue to do this until all your notes are in a line.

8. Once you have all the steps in place, transfer them to a big piece of paper (or a table) that won't be disturbed. Next to each step draw a box that you can put a tick in once that task is complete.

If at any point during this exercise you begin to feel overwhelmed or uncomfortable, just stop. To help relieve any tension, you could try one of the breathing or mindfulness exercises in the book.

This is your plan. And maybe you're not ready to start just yet, but when you are, try to focus only on that first step. And when you have finished, put a tick in its box. Only then move on to the second task. And so on. Respect each task as its own goal, its own achievement. Don't worry if there are big gaps between each one. Take your time.

'You should sit in
meditation for twenty
minutes every day –
unless you're too busy;
then you should sit
for an hour.'

Zen Proverb

Schedule in Enjoyment

Everyone is different and we all enjoy different things. When times become hard or busy, we can forget what brings us happiness. Reminding yourself of these things, and then making a plan for when you'll do them, not only ensures that you actually get to do something you enjoy, but also that you get to look forward to it too.

Make a list on the following pages of activities,
people and places that make you happy or feel good.
They can be big things such as going on holiday or small
things like enjoying a cup of coffee in the sunshine.

Is there something on the list that you could do today,
tomorrow or next week?

Could you work towards making one or two
of these things part of your regular schedule?

Connect With Others

Feeling connected to other people is important. It can help you to feel valued and confident about yourself, and can give you a different perspective on things. Of course, everyone has different social needs. You may be someone who is content with a few close friends or you may need a large group of varied acquaintances to feel satisfied. If you can, try to spend some time connecting with friends or family.

Could you use this time now to call someone or send them a text or email?

Or you might want to make new connections. For example, you could try going to community events where you might have some interests or experiences in common with other people there. Or you could join a group such as a local book club or sports team, or an online community.

If meeting new people feels daunting, perhaps try a class where there is an activity to focus on and you don't need to interact with people until you are more comfortable.

Get Some Green

Research tells us that being in nature is beneficial to our overall wellbeing. This mindfulness exercise will help you reap some of the benefits.

If you can, go outside and find some nature. It might be your back garden, a local park or even a tree on the pavement or a plant growing in the cracks of a wall. If you can't go outside, a house plant will also work, or even just looking out of a window at the sky.

1. Choose something in that environment that you can focus on. It might be the bark of a tree, a flower, a cloud or a few blades of grass in a lawn.

2. Look closely: notice its outline, its colour.

3. Are there details that you hadn't noticed when you were further away from it?

4. Can you touch it? How does it feel? Is it different to what you expected?

5. If you are able to smell it, do so. What smells can you detect?

6. Does it remind you of anything else?

7. As you go, allow each of these discoveries to gently fill your mind.

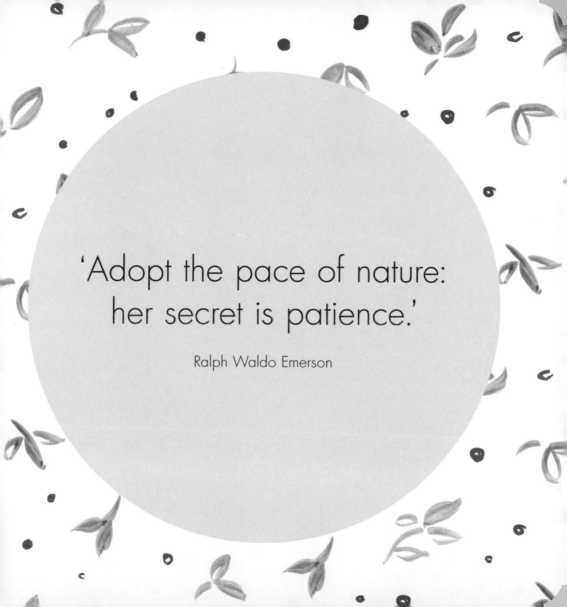

'Adopt the pace of nature:
her secret is patience.'

Ralph Waldo Emerson

Take a Kindness Break #1

Too often, being kind to ourselves gets forgotten, especially when we're busy (and even when we're not), and for some of us it doesn't come naturally or easily. Use this time now to practise being kind to yourself.

Name one thing that you have achieved today. Perhaps it was going on a run, completing a piece of work or even just getting out of bed this morning – remember, we all find different things difficult, and often small things are not small at all. Write it down on the opposite page. Now spend some time thinking about what that achievement means to you and appreciate your own part in getting it done – give yourself a mental pat on the back.

Choose Lunch

How many of us have lunch (or breakfast, or dinner) while
doing something else, or sometimes skip it all together?
If this is you, why not consider scheduling in time to have
a proper lunch break. If you can't make it a whole hour,
instead aim for at least twenty minutes.

When you take your lunch break, stop fully whatever activity
you were in the middle of, and – if you can – take yourself
away from where you were previously busy, ideally
into another room or space.

You could even turn part of your lunch break into
a mindfulness exercise, by really focusing on the tastes
and textures of each mouthful.

For more tips on how to make eating and drinking a mindful
exercise, flip back to 'Mindful Hydration'.

Worked Up

There can be times in our day when we feel worked up and angry. If this is something that you struggle with, why not try some of the techniques below to help you manage your feelings.

Breathe slowly – Try to breathe out for longer than you breathe in, and focus on each breath as you take it.

Relax your body – If you can feel your body getting tense, try focusing on each part of your body in turn, tensing and then relaxing your muscles.

Leave the situation – Just taking a short walk can help you think about the situation, decide how you want to react and feel more in control.

Channel your energy safely – Relieve some of your feelings in a way that doesn't hurt yourself or others. You could try tearing up a newspaper, hitting a pillow or smashing ice cubes in a sink.

Distract yourself – Anything that completely changes your situation, thoughts or patterns can help stop your anger escalating. You could try putting on upbeat music (and dancing along if you like), doing some colouring or taking a cold shower.

Get mindful – Mindfulness techniques can help you become aware of when you're getting angry and help you to calm down. Why not start with the 'Body Scan' exercise that's a few pages ahead.

'Nothing in life is
to be feared, it is only
to be understood.'

Marie Curie

Body Scan

The body scan is a popular mindfulness technique, in which you move your attention slowly through different parts of your body, starting from your toes and moving all the way to the top of your head and then back down again. You could focus on feelings of warmth, tension, tingling or relaxation in different parts of your body. This exercise is best done in a quiet place where you won't be disturbed, but you can do it anywhere.

1.   Sit in a comfortable position, and breathe slowly and deeply.

2.   Start to move your awareness through your body, working upwards from your feet.

3.   Pay attention to the sensations in your toes, feet, legs, back, arms, fingers, shoulders, neck, jaw, eyes, face and scalp.

4.   When you notice tension, pause.

5.   Gradually release this tension as you breathe out and relax. Then move on.

6.   Once you reach your scalp, start to move your attention back down your body in the opposite order, ending with your feet.

7.   When you reach your feet, notice how they feel on the floor. Stay with that feeling for as long as you want to before getting up.

Managing Panic

If you ever feel extremely anxious or experience panic attacks, here are some suggestions for things you can do in that moment to help you cope.

Because it can be hard to remember even simple things at such times, you might want to fold down the corner of the page so that it's ready at hand when you need it. Or you could copy the information on to a separate sheet to keep in your bag or somewhere easily accessible, or perhaps take a picture of it on your phone.

Focus on your breathing – It can help to concentrate on breathing slowly in and out while counting to five.

Stamp on the spot – Some people find this helps them to control their breathing.

Focus on your senses – For example, taste mint-flavoured sweets or gum, or touch or cuddle something soft.

Try grounding techniques – Grounding techniques can help you feel more in control. You could try the 'Stay Grounded' exercise over the page.

Stay Grounded

Grounding techniques can help if you're feeling extremely anxious or distressed, or experiencing a panic attack. They work to keep you connected to the present and help you avoid feelings, memories or intrusive thoughts that you don't feel able to cope with just yet. You could try:

1. Breathing slowly (see the 'Focus on Breathing' exercise earlier in the book).

2. Listening to sounds around you ('Your Daily Orchestra' exercise might help here).

3. Walking barefoot.

4.   Wrapping yourself in a blanket and feeling it
     around you.

5.   Touching something with an interesting or
     appealing texture.

6.   Sniffing something with a strong smell.

The key is to focus your mind on the sensations you are
feeling right now.

You might find it helpful to keep a box of things with different
textures and smells (for example, perfume, a blanket and
some smooth stones) ready for when you may need them.

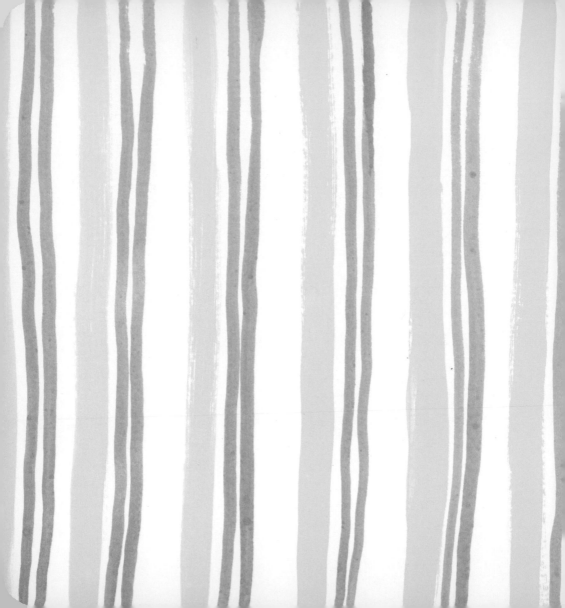

'I'm not afraid of storms,
for I'm learning how
to sail my ship.'

Louisa May Alcott

Barefoot

This is a helpful grounding exercise for when you're feeling worked up, worried or stressed.

1.   Take your shoes and socks off.

2.   While sitting down, place your bare feet flat on the floor roughly hip-width apart.

3.   Notice how the ground feels on the soles of your feet. Which parts of your feet are touching the ground?

4.   If you are able, slowly stand up and feel the pressure on your feet change. Notice how stable you feel, how your feet connect you to the solid ground.

5.   Take two deep breaths.

6.   Now, slowly walk around the room or space you are in. Notice how with each step your weight moves across the surface of your feet. And how each step keeps you stable and upright.

7.   If there is a different sort of flooring nearby, such as a rug, walk over to it. Notice how the change in texture feels on the soles of your feet.

8.   Return to standing still and once again notice how stable you are on your feet.

9.   Take two further deep breaths and finish when you're ready.

Stretch to Destress #3

These two stretches are designed to help relieve tension in your neck, which can lead to headaches as well as tension in your upper back.

Neck Roll

1. Sit or stand with your back straight and plant both feet flat on the floor, roughly hip-width apart.

2. Relax. Notice your breathing for three breaths, then lean your head forward. Don't force it.

3. Slowly roll your head towards the right and hold it for ten seconds or for as long as it is comfortable.

4. Bring your head back to the front, still leaning forward, and repeat the action on the left side.

5. Relax again and lift your head to its normal position.

6. Do this three times in each direction.

Neck Tilt

1. Sit or stand with your back straight and plant both feet flat on the floor, roughly hip-width apart.

2. Bring your right arm up and clasp the top of your head.

3. Gently pull your head towards your right shoulder until you feel a light stretch.

4. Hold the position for ten to fifteen seconds or for however long you feel comfortable.

5. Now slowly bring your head back to the upright position and bring your arm back down to your side.

6. Repeat the process on the other side.

Your Daily Orchestra

At any one time we can be surrounded by a huge variety of sounds, but we don't often pay them much attention.

Take a moment now to sit quietly for five minutes (or longer if you can manage) and really listen to what sounds you can hear. Try to separate out the different strands. The longer you listen, the more sounds you'll be able to pick out. You may be surprised by how many different sources of sound you can distinguish.

When you have finished, spend a minute or two appreciating the amazing job your brain does, because while you may not be paying any attention, your background mind is constantly sifting through these different sounds, and assessing whether you may need to respond to them. Thanks brain.

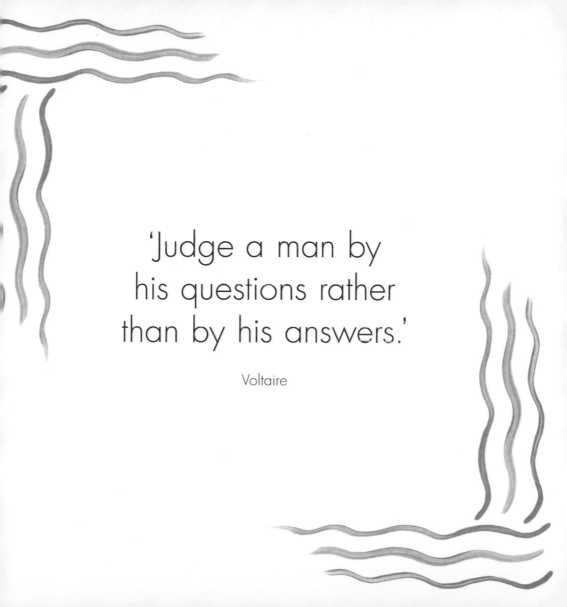

'Judge a man by
his questions rather
than by his answers.'

Voltaire

Take a Kindness Break #2

None of us achieves all our goals, and everyone makes mistakes. In fact, it's an important part of what makes us human. But it can be hard to remember this when we're under pressure, and we can often be unkind to ourselves when we don't meet our expectations.

Is there a way in which you tend to judge yourself harshly? Imagine now that a close friend or someone you care about told you that they did the same thing. What would you say to them to be supportive and comforting? Write it down opposite. Now read it aloud or in your head as if you were telling yourself.

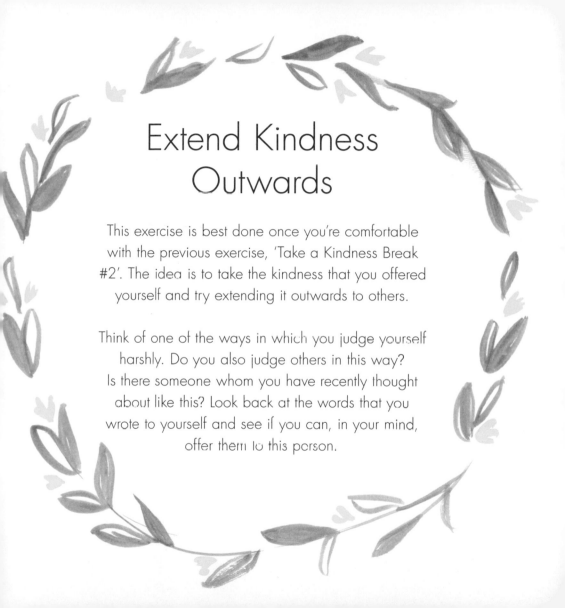

Extend Kindness Outwards

This exercise is best done once you're comfortable with the previous exercise, 'Take a Kindness Break #2'. The idea is to take the kindness that you offered yourself and try extending it outwards to others.

Think of one of the ways in which you judge yourself harshly. Do you also judge others in this way? Is there someone whom you have recently thought about like this? Look back at the words that you wrote to yourself and see if you can, in your mind, offer them to this person.

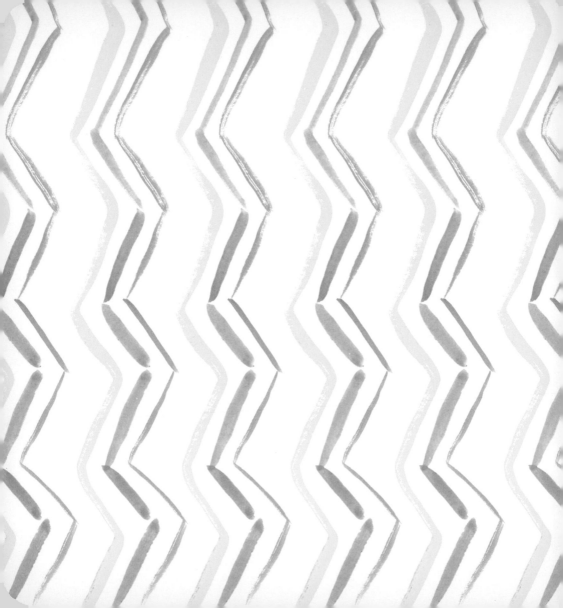

'Be kind to yourself ...
You will come to see
that all evolves us.'

Rumi

Kindness Reminder

It can be hard to remember to challenge that harsh internal voice when it gets going – and for many people it's often just left on in the background, giving a constant critical narrative as we go about our day. Having a physical reminder can be a useful nudge to actively check that voice, and offer ourselves some compassionate and kind words instead.

What image represents kindness to you? It could be an animal or a plant, or just a pattern, symbol or colour. Try drawing it on the following pages. You might come up with lots of images, in which case draw as many as you want.

Now get a pad of sticky notes and copy that image (or images) onto a handful of them. Then attach those sticky notes to places where you feel you could do with a reminder to be kind to yourself. For instance, beside your bed, next to your front door or on your computer.

Create

Whether it's knitting, painting, doodling, carpentry or making a Lego model, exercising our creativity can be a great way to relax and give our mind space to stretch.

As an adult there can seem to be fewer opportunities to be creative, so consider what might work for you and try out a few different things. Even just ten minutes spent being creative can make a big difference.

It may be worth thinking about something creative that you could easily do when you're on the go. And if you want to try something now, why not start with the 'Doodle' exercise on the following page.

Doodle

Don't think about it, just do it.

This isn't about creating a work of art (no one but you will see it anyway), and it needn't be a thoughtful expression of your innermost feelings. With doodling it's the process that's the point. Just making simple marks on paper can offer your mind a break and an outlet.

Pick up a pen, pencil, crayon, eyeliner or whatever you've got that will make a mark. Place the tip on the paper over the page and move it in any direction you want. Now keep moving it for between one and five minutes. Don't worry about what picture or design you're making, just keep going.

'A lion chased me up a tree, and I greatly enjoyed the view from the top.'

Confucius

Stretch to Destress #4

This twisting stretch focuses on your lower back and you needn't push hard to feel the stretch working.

1. Sit on a chair with your back straight and plant both feet flat on the floor, roughly hip-width apart.

2. Keeping your back straight (i.e., not bent over) and your hips facing forward, gently rotate your torso and shoulders towards the right.

3. Remember: only twist as far as is comfortable.

4. Hold the position for ten to thirty seconds, and then repeat on the other side.

If you have a bit more time, why not try all four of the stretching exercises in this book one after another.

Anti-Social Media?

Social media can be a great way to stay in touch with people, find out what's going on in the world and share our interests. But many people are finding that aspects of social media have a negative effect on their wellbeing. For instance, we can compare how we see our lives (often focusing on our perceived flaws) with how we see the lives of others, forgetting that what we see on screen can be far from the truth.

It may be useful to consider the impact social media has on you. How does it make you feel when you use it? After you use it? Do certain habits have a positive impact (maybe messaging friends), while others have a negative impact (such as scrolling through status updates)?

Being conscious of how our online habits influence how we feel can help us make decisions that better support our wellbeing.

'Everything flows
and nothing abides;
everything gives way and
nothing stays fixed.'

Heraclitus

Make a Change

Making a change can help bring a fresh awareness to your everyday world. And the change needn't be anything drastic. It could be tweaking your regular habits or altering the space around you. For instance, even just varying your route to work or to the shops can help you to be more mindful of your environment and enjoy being in the present.

Is there something that you could do right now?
Could you perhaps rearrange the room that you're in?
Or even just reorganize your desk (a good tidy-up could also do the trick)?

Could you do something different in your next break? Maybe you could take a walk outside or visit a new place for lunch?

Play Time

When children play, they do it for sheer pleasure.
They are not trying to achieve anything or to reach
a particular goal, and there's not necessarily anything
to show for it when they have finished. Rather, they do
it because they enjoy *doing* it. Just that. Nothing else.

Is there anything that you enjoy (or perhaps used to enjoy) *doing*? Perhaps it's reading or listening to music, chatting to friends or watching your favourite film, fishing or walking.

Give yourself some time now to think about what you enjoy *doing* and make a note of what comes to mind on the following page. When might you be able to do it next?

'May you live
all the days
of your life.'

Jonathan Swift

Resources

For information and support,
you can contact the Mind Infoline.

Phone: 0300 123 3393
Text: 86463
Monday to Friday, 9am to 6pm
(except for bank holidays).

Or email: info@mind.org.uk

You can find additional resources on the
Mind website at mind.org.uk.

For support and advice in your area,
find your local Mind at mind.org.uk/localmind.

Elefriends is a supportive online community, run by Mind,
where you can be yourself. It's a safe place to listen, share
and be heard. You can sign up at www.elefriends.org.uk.

If you are feeling overwhelmed or need a listening ear,
we recommend contacting Samaritans.

Phone: 116 123
24 hours a day, 365 days a year.

If you enjoyed *Take a Moment,* you might also want to check out ...

THE WELLBEING JOURNAL

Creative Activities to Inspire

Explore your inner world and discover how creativity and reflection can have a powerful positive influence on your life.

In aid of

mind
for better mental health

978-1-78243-800-7 in paperback format